World Cuisine | **Morocco**

# Morocco

**With dishes by:**

Mohamed Fedal • Frédéric Fétiveau • Fatéma Hal

World Cuisine

WORLD CUISINE - **Morocco**

Coordination: ESP Promotions Ltd, London
And TP& Associates, Madrid and Milan

For further information on the collection or to purchase
any books that you have missed, please visit:
www.timesonline.co.uk/cookbooks

For further information regarding publication rights,
please contact: cookbookinfo@gmail.com

© Ciro Ediciones, S.A., Barcelone

*Original idea*
Jaume Fàbregas

*Editorial director*
Juan Manuel Bellver

*Collection coordinator*
Núria Egido

*Culinary advisors*
Xavier Agulló
R. de Nola
Jorge Osés Labadie

*Editors*
Mercè Bolló
Pau Raya Castell
Miguel Ángel Sánchez

*Contributing editors*
Esther Buira
Lola Hernández
M.ª Dolores Escudero
David Ibáñez
Carles Llurda
Meritxell Piqué
Carles Raventós

*Photography*
Christian M. Kempin / Gastrofotos
Daniel Loewe / Joan Jolis, S.L.
Yvan Zedda
Leonardo Antoniabis
Marisa Pérez
Manuel Raya

*Layout*
New Color Book, S.L.

*Cover design*
WEP Milano

*Preprint*
Digitalscreen

*Printers*
Avenida Gráfica

ISBN 84-609-7351-4 (complete works)
ISBN 84-609-7355-7 (volume III – Morocco)
Legal deposit: M-39744-2005

© of photographs, introduction and drinks: Stock Photos, Agencia Cover

# Contents

To whet the appetite

## An oasis of taste

When I arrived, hot and thirsty, in Morocco I ordered a mint tea at the first little café that I stumbled across. I was left dumbfounded by the sweet discovery and intoxication of mint and orange blossom aromas. It was from that moment that my fascination with this extraordinary country began. It inspired a journey through multi-coloured markets, all abounding in a rich and varied selection of fresh vegetables  which are so important in Moroccan cuisine.

Moroccan cuisine is steeped in history yet it is exceptionally contemporary in form: it is light and healthy, which suits the demands of our fast paced and fashion conscious world. Moroccan cuisine is versatile and is ideal for special occasions as well as every day life. It is a cuisine characterised by slow cooking, generous but not overwhelming in its use of spices or sauces; all these

combine to facilitate the unique pleasure of eating the food with your fingers!! Tasty lamb is perhaps most commonly cooked and is used in *tajines* and for *mechoui*, the names come from the pots used for their cooking, served with mounds of couscous and garnished with pickled lemons, herbs and plenty of olives, and illuminated by colourful spices. As well as the lamb, there is of course a great deal of fresh fish.

And then there are the thousands of layers of *filo*, the Arabesque pastry that combines almonds, sumptuous honey and dates, 'little fingers of the desert'.

The following succulent recipes will transport you to this exotic, fascinating and boundless country with an outstanding cuisine, and one that ends with a simple glass of mint tea.

# World Cuisine: Morocco

Marked by religious doctrine, diverse civilisations and the omnipresent legacy of the Berbers, Moroccan cuisine has become one of the most fascinating foods of all for the western palate. Its rich variety of stews and refined use of spices, the marriage of conflicting tastes and a delicious array of sweets, all define Moroccan cuisine, a cuisine that abounds in true Mediterranean essence.

The countries of North Africa, including Morocco, Algeria, Tunisia, Libya and Mauritania, have always been desirable targets for conquering civilisations. Yet amidst centuries of invasion, the indigenous Berber people have been notoriously resistant; their inhospitable lands, like those of the Sahara, have helped keep their traditions alive.

The survival of Berber cuisine, from where honey, beans, lentils and wheat originate, is one the greatest displays of its tenacity. Despite the importance that Berber cuisine plays in Moroccan food, the influence of other countries should not be ignored. Arab influence, for example, brought with it the Persian love of spices, nuts and dates, a love for sweet foods, and a fondness for combining flavours. And Moroccan cuisine has also been shaped by the influence of Islam, the country's main religion. The prohibition of pork or alcohol, or the obligation of Muslims to fast during the month of Ramadan, has helped shape Morocco's culinary customs.

With an overtly rich cultural mix and the importance of religion in daily Moroccan life, it is especially commendable that Berber cuisine has survived today. Couscous is a native Berber dish, where couscous is steamed and topped with a rich stew of meat and vegetables, chicken or fish. Another Berber speciality is the *tajine*, a stew of meat and vegetables, and the *harira*, a thick and nutritious broth that is eaten to mark the end of fasting. During this period, Muslims renew their relationship with God through abstaining from eating, drinking, smoking and sexual relations, from dawn to dusk. As well as *harira*, *beghrir*, a type of pancake served with honey, is eaten when the period of fasting is complete, and special cakes fried in oil and covered in honey (*shebbakia*) are also common. Bread, *khbuz*, is another fundamental element of Moroccan cookery, and is baked at home with wholemeal flour or a mixture of barley and wheat flour. Bread can be served to accompany a main course, or is eaten alone at breakfast, where it is

dunked in olive oil or spread with honey.

As well as traditional cookery and the importance of religion in all aspects of Moroccan daily life, shopping in town markets, where colourful spices such as cayenne pepper, paprika, ginger, cinnamon, cumin, coriander and saffron are on offer, takes on a distinct social role with interchange of money and banter. One of the best-known spice mixtures is *ras el-hanout*, a generic name given to a particular combination of spices used by different cooks. A whole array of tempting snacks can be sampled at street stalls, including *kefta*, diced and spiced lamb with salad and hot sauce. All wrapped in bread. It is also common to find roast chicken served with French fries.

Chicken is, along with lamb, the most commonly eaten meat. It can be spit-roasted, used in *tajines*, couscous or *pastilla* - a sumptuous mixture of shredded meat and almonds. Lamb is the main ingredient in *m'choui*, where meat is roasted or baked slowly, and *touajen* is a marinated stew with chicken, lamb or fish. To finish off a meal, or at any other time of day and to accompany a glass of mint tea, Moroccans are particularly fond of cakes and sweets, often made with marzipan or pistachios. Furthermore, citrus fruits, figs, apricots, melons and plums, are grown everywhere in Morocco, and are often used in salads or *tajines*. But without doubt, the most characteristic of all Moroccan fruit is the date, which can be eaten as an appetiser, served in stews, or used in desserts. The abundance of ingredients, the delicate use of spices, its delicious desserts and the importance that food plays in Moroccan daily life, are just some of the tempting reasons to delve further into this fascinating and delicious cuisine.

World Cuisine

# Starters

This collection of traditional dishes
has been created by:

**Frédéric Fétiveau**
Restaurant Medina de Braganza
and Café Oliver

# Salata al-laymun al-marqad bi-milh wa bi-l-fulful
## Salad of salted lemon and peppers

Level of difficulty: low
Preparation time: 35 minutes

**Serves 4**
*200g green peppers*
*200g red peppers*
*1 onion*
*2 lemons*
*1/2 small cup lemon juice*
*1/2 small cup orange juice*
*10g garlic*
*5g cumin*
*Black olives*
*Oil*
*Salt*

To prepare the salted lemon (which takes fifteen days), cut the two ends off the lemon, make an incision in both sides of the lemon in the form of a cross, rub in plenty of salt and leave to penetrate. Keep for two weeks at room temperature, if possible in a sealed container.

Wash the peppers and roast with the onion in a pre-heated 220°C oven for one hour. Remove. Peel the vegetables, cut the pepper into strips and chop the onion. Place the orange and lemon juice in a saucepan over medium heat and reduce. Add the peppers, onion, a little garlic that has been previously sliced and sautéed, and the cumin. Cook quickly and remove from the heat.

The pepper salad is served cold or warm with strips of salted lemon and black olives. Drizzle with olive oil.

This is a refreshing salad with the unmistakeable and typically Moroccan taste of salted lemon. Another way to prepare the lemon is to cut it into strips, rub with salt, and then assemble it together again, leaving the lemon in an air-tight container for two weeks.

Level of difficulty: low
Preparation time: 15 minutes

# Salata al-jiyar wa-l-tut al-ard
# Gherkin and strawberry salad

**Serves 4**
*250g strawberries*
*150g gherkins*
*100g dates*
*100g fresh figs*
*1 pot plain yoghurt*
*50g honey*
*Mint*
*Spring onion*

Chop the gherkins, dates and figs and place in a dish. Wash the strawberries and slice. Add to the salad with finely chopped mint. Next, mix the honey and yoghurt thoroughly. Pour over the other ingredients. Finally, decorate with chopped spring onion, more chopped dates and sliced strawberries.

This unusual taste combination is surprisingly delicious. Chopped fresh cucumber may be used instead of gherkin in the recipe.

## *Tabulé*
## Tabbouleh salad

Level of difficulty: low
Preparation time: 15 minutes

**Serves 4**
*300g bulgar wheat*
*100g onion, finely chopped*
*200g tomatoes, finely chopped*
*50g raisins*
*5g mint, finely chopped finely*
*5g coriander, finely chopped*
*5g parsley, finely chopped*
*150ml lemon juice*

Place bulgar wheat in bowl and add enough boiling water just to cover. Cover with clingfilm and leave to steam for 20 minutes. Add the onion, raisins, tomatoes, coriander, mint and parsley. Drizzle with lemon juice and leave to rest for a minimum of three hours or if possible, half a day.

Level of difficulty: low
Preparation time: 20 minutes
Cooking time: 40 minutes

# *Hummus*

# Hummus

**Serves 4**
*150g chickpeas*
*100g onion*
*2 tablespoons tahini paste*
*Coriander*
*Olive oil*
*Lemon juice*
*4 pitta breads*

Soak the chickpeas overnight in water. Place in a pan with a little water, a dash of olive oil, the onion and coriander. Simmer for 40 minutes or until the chickpeas are soft. Next, remove the onion and coriander, drain the chickpeas (keeping back a little of the stock) and mash with a fork or pulse in a blender to a thick paste, adding a little stock if necessary. Add the *tahini* and lemon juice. Blend. Sprinkle with a little chopped fresh coriander and drizzle with oil. Serve with hot pitta bread.

*Tahini*, or toasted sesame paste, is available from health food shops and some supermarkets. Rich in calcium, phosphorous and vegetable proteins, it is often used in Morocco for salad dressings and as an accompaniment to vegetables. If using tinned chickpeas there is no need to soak or cook them.

Level of difficulty: low
Preparation time: 15 minutes
Cooking time: 5 minutes

# *Laffa badinyan*
# Aubergine rolls

**Serves 4**
*250g aubergines*
*250g ground almonds*
*500ml orange flower water*
*1 tablespoon ground cinnamon*
*Oil*
*Sesame seeds (optional)*
*Honey*

Firstly, mix the almonds and ground cinnamon. Add the orange flower water little by little until an even and creamy consistency has been obtained. Next, slice the aubergines lengthways and fry in a pan until soft. Remove from the pan and place on absorbent kitchen paper to remove the excess fat. Fill the aubergine strips with the almond paste and roll into a sausage shape. Place on a dish and drizzle with honey. To finish, sprinkle with sesame seeds.

These exquisite aubergine bites could be considered as a modern-day equivalent of the traditional pastilla. Concocted by Mohamed Fadel, they now form part of the national cuisine.

Level of difficulty: low
Preparation time: 20 minutes
Cooking time: 15 minutes

# Kefta bi-l-warda

# Meatballs with rose petals

**Serves 4**
*300g minced beef*
*200g minced lamb*
*100g onion*
*3 eggs*
*50g ginger*
*20g chopped garlic*
*1 tablespoon cumin*
*4 tablespoons oil*
*2 tablespoons* ras el hanout
*2 teaspoons rose water*
*Petals of 1 rose*
*Oil*
*Salt*
*Pepper*

Mix the meats, eggs, chopped garlic, onion and ginger. Season with salt and pepper, add the cumin and *ras el hanout*. Work together until thoroughly mixed, add the rose water, finely chopped rose petals and leave to marinade for at least thirty minutes to allow the meat to infuse with the flavours. Next, shape the mixture into small balls, lightly flatten and fry in oil until golden.

*Ras el hanout* literally means "the best in the shop". You could substitute a mild curry powder for a less complex effect.

Level of difficulty: high
Preparation time: 40 minutes
Cooking time: 10 minutes

# Briouat yaban
## Cheese parcels

**Serves 4**
1 packet filo *pastry*
1 egg
100g Roquefort cheese
300g whipping cream
400g goat's cheese
90ml single cream
50g raisins
Spring onion, chopped
Olive oil
Salt
Icing sugar (optional)

Beat together the Roquefort cheese and the whipping cream until an even paste has been formed. Set aside. Beat 200g goat's cheese with the single cream and when smooth, add the raisins. Set aside. Thirdly, mix the other half of goat's cheese with some oil, add the spring onion and set aside.

Next, cut the *filo* pastry into squares of roughly four-centimetres. Place a small amount of the Roquefort mixture onto one end of some of the squares, and fold over to form into a triangular shape. Seal. Brush the upper-most sheet with a little beaten egg. Now add a spoonful of goat's cheese mixture into the centre of other *filo* pastry squares. Fold over the two sides so the filling does not spill out, and bring the two ends together to create a circular *briouat*. Brush with beaten egg. Finally, fill the remaining squares with the goat's cheese and spring onion mixture, roll up to form a cigar-shaped finger. Brush with egg. When all the *briouats* have been prepared, fry in hot oil until golden and sprinkle (optional) with a little icing sugar.

*Briouats* are one of the best-loved and most common appetizers in Morocco. The fillings, sweet or savoury, are as varied as the distinct shapes of these delicious pastry snacks.

# Kefta wa-l briouat
# Beef parcels with lamb and chicken meatballs

Level of difficulty: high
Preparation time: 40 minutes
Cooking time: 15 minutes

Serves 4

For the *keftas* (meatballs):
300g minced beef
200g minced lamb
100g onion
4g salt
6g pepper
20g garlic, chopped
50g ginger, chopped
40g ground cumin
4 tablespoons oil
2 tablespoons ras el hanout
1 handful coriander
3 eggs

For the chicken *briouats:*
1 packet filo pastry
1 chicken breast, minced
100g onion
1 garlic clove, chopped
50g raisins
100ml olive oil
1 egg
Cinnamon
Sugar teaspoon
Saffron (a pinch)

To make the *kefta*, mix the meats with the egg, garlic, onion and ginger. Season and add the spices. When it is mixed thoroughly, start to form into small balls by hand. Fry in oil until golden.

To make the *briouats*, sauté the onion and chopped garlic in a saucepan. When golden, add the minced chicken breast, cinnamon, sugar, a little saffron and raisins and fry lightly so the meat becomes impregnated with the aromas. Cut the *filo* pastry into squares of roughly four-centimetres. Place a little of the meat mixture into one corner of the *filo* pastry and fold over to make a triangle. Brush with a little beaten egg, fry in hot oil and sprinkle with icing sugar.

*Kefta* or *kofta* is an Arabic word that literally means minced meat. These delicious meatballs may be prepared with one type of meat or a mixture of several. *Kefta briouats* can also be made.

Level of difficulty: low
Preparation time: 20 minutes
Cooking time: 5 minutes

# *Qishda al-yulban*
# Cream of pea soup

**Serves 4**
*400g peas*
*100g onion, finely chopped*
*1/2 l chicken stock*
*100ml single cream*
*Salt*
*Mint, chopped*

Heat some oil in a saucepan and sauté the onion. When golden, add the peas and mint to taste. Next add enough chicken stock to cover the peas and leave to cook for five minutes. Now, remove from the heat, add the butter and single cream, and blend in a food processor until smooth. Season. Finally, pass through a fine sieve. Decorate with peas and a few mint leaves or simply sprinkle with chopped mint.

It is important that the peas are not overcooked so that the soup maintains its distinctive green colour. If the peas are over-cooked, the soup can take on a brownish hue.

Level of difficulty: low
Preparation time: 20 minutes
Cooking time: 15 minutes

# *Qishda al-qara'a*
# Cream of pumpkin soup

**Serves 4**
*500g pumpkin*
*200g onion*
*1 l chicken stock*
*100g single cream*
*50g butter*
*Olive oil*
*Salt*

Finely chop the onion and lightly fry in olive oil until soft and translucent. Add the peeled and chopped pumpkin and continue frying. Now add enough chicken stock to cover the ingredients, and leave to cook for between ten to fifteen minutes. Remove the saucepan from the heat, add the butter and single cream and blend until smooth. Season with salt and pepper, then press through a sieve. Serve hot, drizzle with olive oil and sprinkle with black sesame seeds.

# Shorba bi-l-judar wa kefta faraj al-hamman
## Vegetable soup with pigeon meatballs

Level of difficulty: medium
Preparation time: 30 minutes
Cooking time: 30 minutes

**Serves 4**
1 pigeon
1 l chicken stock
300g potatoes
200g carrots
200g onion
200g courgettes
200g pumpkin
150g leeks
100g celery
20g chopped garlic
3 eggs
1 bunch coriander
Salt
Pepper

Chop the onion, garlic and coriander. Mix together. Remove the flesh from the pigeon, finely chop the meat and mix with half the onion and garlic mixture. Season with salt and pepper. Form the mixture into small balls (*kefta*). Meanwhile, fry the pigeon carcass in oil and add the remaining garlic, onion and coriander. When golden, add the diced carrots, potatoes, leeks, celery, courgettes and pumpkin, the chicken stock and the prepared pigeon *keftas*. Cook over a medium heat until the vegetables are tender. Before serving, remove the carcass. Break the eggs, beat well and add to the hot soup.

*Chorba* is the generic name for thick Arabic soup. The exquisite pigeon meatballs complement this basic recipe to perfection.

Level of difficulty: low
Preparation time: 30 minutes
Cooking time: 15 minutes

# Shorba al-dayay bi-l-yaus
# Chicken and walnut soup

**Serves 4**
*400g chicken*
*150g walnuts*
*200g onions*
*40g ginger*
*20g garlic*
*Chicken stock*
*Salt*
*Pepper*
*Saffron*
*Oil*
*Coriander*
*Parsley*

Heat some oil in a saucepan. Fry the finely chopped garlic and onion until golden. Add the chicken cut into large pieces, the saffron, cumin, ginger, chopped coriander, salt and pepper. Mix well to allow the meat to infuse with the flavours. Add enough chicken stock to cover the ingredients and leave to cook for approximately fifteen minutes over a low heat. Toast the walnuts on aluminium foil in the oven. Just before serving, add the toasted walnuts.

Walnuts are the perfect accompaniment to this delicious seasoned soup, although they may be replaced with dried fruits, to suit individual taste preferences.

Level of difficulty: medium
Preparation time: 45 minutes
Cooking time: 35 minutes

# *Al-harira*
# Moroccan potage

**Serves 4**
*300g minced lamb*
*150g lentils*
*100g onion, finely chopped*
*100g rice*
*300g tomatoes, chopped*
*50g ginger*
*2 parsley sprigs, chopped*
*50g celery*
*10g cinnamon*
*10g paprika*
*10g cumin*
*50g flour*
*5g salt*
*5g ground pepper*
*1.5 litres water*
*2 eggs*
*Coriander*
*Oil*

Heat a little oil in a saucepan, add the onion and celery. Fry until golden. Now add the minced lamb, coriander, salt, pepper, spices, a little water and cook for approximately 15 minutes. Add the chopped tomatoes, parsley and lentils, and cook for a further 20 minutes on a low heat, adding water if necessary. Add the rice and when cooked, pour in the beaten eggs. Finally, add the flour that has been previously mixed with a little water, and stir continually to avoid it from sticking to the bottom of the pan.

It could be said that *harira* is Morocco's national soup, especially during the month of Ramadan. Although each cook has his or her own variation of the recipe, lentils and chickpeas are commonly used.

World Cuisine

# Main courses

Level of difficulty: low
Preparation time: 20 minutes
Cooking time: 40 minutes

# Tayin al-jaruf bi-l-barquq al-sabit wa-l-laus
# Lamb *tajine* with prunes and almonds

**Serves 4**
*1 small leg spring lamb*
*400g prunes*
*200g almonds*
*200g onions*
*100g ginger*
*100ml oil*
*1g saffron*
*4 garlic cloves*
*Meat stock*
*1 pinch of coriander*
*1 pinch of parsley*
*Salt*
*Honey*

Lightly fry the chopped garlic and onion in a *tajine* cooking pot or saucepan. When golden, add the finely chopped ginger, coriander and parsley. Now add the saffron and legs of lamb. Fry lightly for a few more minutes and then cover with meat stock. Leave over a low heat. When the meat is tender, remove from the heat and pulse the remaining ingredients to make the sauce. Return the meat and sauce to the saucepan, add the quantity of prunes and honey desired and cook for five minutes. Just before serving, fry the almonds in a little oil and add to the stew.

Contrasting meat, prune and almond flavours are typically Moroccan; this dish is one of the most popular.

Level of difficulty: low
Preparation time: 15 minutes
Cooking time: 30 minutes

# Tayin dayay taryd
## Chicken *filo* tajine

**Serves 4**

*1kg chicken, cubed, salted and fried*
*100g onion*
*20g garlic*
*20g ginger, chopped finely*
*1g saffron*
*1/2 handful coriander, chopped finely*
*1/2 handful parsley, chopped finely*
*Water*
*Salt*

**For the *filo* crackers:**
*1/2 l water*
*500g flour*
*1 egg*
*Salt*
*Oil*

Poach the garlic and onion in a little oil in a *tajine*, and when golden, add the saffron, coriander, parsley, ginger and fried chicken. Cover with water and leave to cook until the meat is tender and succulent.

For the crackers, blend the water, egg, flour, pinch of salt and work together. Add the oil little by little until an elastic and malleable paste has been formed. Make into small balls and roll out finely to form crepe-like circles. Lightly toast on both sides in a frying pan without oil. Remove from the heat, break up and then place in a dish. Place the chicken *tajine* over the crackers and spoon over some meat juices.

Level of difficulty: medium
Preparation time: 40 minutes
Cooking time: 35 minutes

# Tayin juruf bi-salabiat al-yasr
# Lamb *tajine* with carrot fritters

**Serves 4**
*1.2kg lamb, cubed*
*200g onion, chopped finely*
*10g garlic, chopped finely*
*1g saffron*
*Lamb stock (optional)*
*Parsley*

**For the fritters:**
*300g carrot*
*10g garlic, chopped*
*2 eggs*
*1 teaspoon ground cumin*
*1 tablespoon flour*
*Coriander, chopped*

Heat a little oil in a saucepan or *tajine* and fry the garlic and onion until golden. Add the lamb, cut into cubes of one-centimetre, saffron, chopped parsley and cover with lamb stock or water. Leave to cook for about 25 minutes, until the meat is tender.

Meanwhile, prepare the fritters. Sauté the garlic and coriander in an oiled frying pan, add the cumin and carrots, previously blanched in hot water, and cut into fine strips. Remove from the heat and set aside. Mix the flour and eggs in a bowl to a semi-liquid paste, add the carrot mixture and now shape into balls. Drop into a hot and oiled frying pan until golden and crispy.

If the fritter paste is too dry, add a little water. The fritters are normally added to the *tajine* at the end of cooking, but if you prefer them crispy, then they can be placed on top of the meat just before serving.

Level of difficulty: low
Preparation time: 35 minutes
Cooking time: 20 minutes

# Tayin samak al-maryan bi-l-janyabil
## Bream with ginger

**Serves 4**
1.2kg bream
200g black olives
200g preserved salted lemons
2g saffron
3 large tomatoes
2 onions
4 garlic cloves
Tomatoes
Fish stock or water
Coriander
Parsley
Water

Heat some oil in a *tajine* cooking pot or saucepan. Add the garlic and chopped onions and lightly fry. When golden, add the ginger, coriander, finely chopped parsley and saffron. Clean the bream, cut the fish into three pieces and add to the saucepan along with the quartered tomatoes. Cover with water or fish stock. Leave to cook until the bream is tender. Finally, just before cooking is complete, add the olives and wedges of preserved salted lemon (see *Salad of salted lemon and peppers*).

Although the recipe is tastier with the unmistakable flavour of preserved salted lemon, natural lemon wedges may be used as an alternative. In addition, diced potatoes may be used instead of tomatoes; the stew will still taste excellent.

Level of difficulty: medium
Preparation time: 30 minutes
Cooking time: 20 minutes

# Al-cuscus bi-l-judar al-mausim
# Couscous with seasonal vegetables

Serves 4
100g pumpkin
100g courgette
75g aubergine
75g carrot
75g turnip
Oil

**For the couscous:**
300g couscous
1 teaspoon salt
20g butter
3 glasses water

**For the vegetable stock:**
2 carrots
100g turnip
1 leek
1 aubergine
1 bay leaf
1 sprig thyme
Ginger, parsley and coriander

**For the onion compote**
150g onion
50g raisins
2 tablespoons honey
1 teaspoon ground cinnamon

Place the couscous and salt in a bowl and pour over 500ml of boiling water. Cover and leave for 5 minutes. Transfer to a steamer (or colander set over boiling water), add the butter, cover and steam for 6 to 7 minutes.

Cut the pumpkin, courgette, carrots and turnips into strips and boil until just cooked. Set aside. Cut the aubergine into cubes, place in an oiled frying pan. When golden, remove from the heat and place on absorbent kitchen paper.

To prepare the onion compote, poach the chopped onion in a frying pan in oil. When golden, add the cinnamon, honey, raisins and leave to reduce to a caramelised compote. Assemble the couscous in the centre of the dish and arrange the vegetables on top. Add the aubergine fingers and crown with the onion compote.

---

The word couscous comes from the Berber word *seksu*, and does not refer to the grain itself but rather to the mud or metal dish used for cooking, which is filled with small holes needed for steaming.

Level of difficulty: medium
Preparation time: 1 hour
Cooking time: 40 minutes

# Al-cuscus al-taqlidí
## Couscous Café Oliver

**Serves 4**
*600g chicken, cubed*
*600g lamb, cubed*
*200g chickpeas, soaked*
*overnight*
*150g pumpkin*
*200g carrots*
*200g courgettes*
*200g turnips*
*4 sausages*
*4 meatballs* (kefta)
*1 handful mint*
*1g saffron*
*20g cumin*
*Oil*
*Salt*

**For the onion compote:**
*150g onion*
*50g raisins*
*2 tablespoons honey*
*1 teaspoon ground cinnamon*

**For the couscous:**
*300g couscous*
*20g butter*
*1 teaspoon salt*
*3 glasses water*

Firstly, prepare the couscous (see *Couscous with seasonal vegetables*), adding the chopped pumpkin, carrots and courgette to the vegetable stock. Meanwhile, cook the chicken in a pan with a little water and the mint. In another pan, cook the lamb, water and saffron. Fry the sausages and meatballs in oil. Boil the chickpeas with the cumin. Prepare the onion compote (see *Couscous with seasonal vegetables*), and when the different ingredients are ready, place the couscous in a mound in the centre of a dish, cover with the vegetables, chickpeas and meat.

This meat and vegetable couscous is perhaps the richest, best known and most popular couscous in Morocco and abroad.

# Al-cuscus bi-l-qudban al-mutanawi'at
## Couscous with assorted kebabs

Level of difficulty: medium
Preparation time: 1 hour
Cooking time: 20 minutes

Serves 4
**For the beef kebabs:**
*400g beef loin*
*150g red peppers*

**For the chicken kebabs:**
*2 chicken breasts*
*Juice of 1 lemon*
*1 teaspoon paprika*
*1 teaspoon cumin*
*1 teaspoon chopped coriander*
*1 teaspoon oil*

**For the langoustine kebabs:**
*12 langoustines*

**For the vegetable kebabs:**
*Aubergines*
*Courgettes*
*Carrots*
*Red peppers*
*Green peppers*
*Coriander*

**For the couscous:**
*300g couscous*
*20g butter*
*1 teaspoon salt*
*3 glasses water*

Leave the cubed chicken to marinate in lemon juice, spices and coriander for twelve hours. Prepare the couscous (see *Couscous with seasonal vegetables*). Now prepare the assorted kebabs. For the beef kebabs, cut the meat into mouth-size cubes, season and fry in oil. Assemble the kebabs by alternating with chunks of roasted red pepper. Fry the marinated chicken and again, layer with peppers. For the langoustine brochette, peel the tails, sauté and place three pieces onto each kebab. Finally, boil the vegetables in salted water, drain, cut into cubes and arrange onto four other kebabs.

Now arrange on the plate with the couscous in the centre. Place the kebabs around the couscous. Finally, spoon some cooking stock over the dish.

## Al-cuscus bi-l-sardin wa-l-zaum
# Couscous with sardines and garlic

Level of difficulty: medium
Preparation time: 45 minutes
Cooking time: 30 minutes

Serves 4
1kg sardines
200g shallots
1 bunch young garlic heads
Parsley
Salt

**For the couscous:**
300g couscous
20g butter
1 teaspoon salt
3 glasses water

**For the vegetable stock:**
2 carrots
100g radish
1 leek
1 courgette
1 bay leaf
1 sprig thyme
Ginger
Parsley
Coriander

Prepare the couscous (see *Couscous with seasonal vegetables*). Clean the sardines thoroughly. Roast, preferably on the grill, turning them periodically. Season well. Meanwhile, sauté the sliced garlic heads and shallots until golden. Place the couscous into the centre of a dish and arrange the roasted sardines, garlic and onion on top. Drizzle with the prepared vegetable stock (see above).

Although fish couscous is not as popular as the meat and vegetable varieties of the dish, couscous combines perfectly with fish and seafood flavours.

# *Al-cuscus bi-saratan al-nahr wa-l-qar'a*
# Couscous with crayfish and pumpkin

Level of difficulty: low
Preparation time: 20 minutes
Cooking time: 20 minutes

Serves 4
1kg crayfish
200g pumpkin
1 garlic clove
Parsley
Butter
Salt

For the couscous:
300g couscous
20g butter
1 teaspoon salt
3 glasses water

For the vegetable stock:
2 carrots
100g radish
1 leek
1 courgette
1 bay leaf
1 sprig thyme
Ginger
Parsley
Coriander

Bring a pan of salted water to the boil. Add the crayfish and boil for about four minutes. Do not overcook. Carefully remove the tails so that the head and claws remain in tact. Sauté in butter with a clove of chopped garlic and chopped parsley. Next, peel the pumpkin, boil in salted water for ten minutes and cut into crescent shapes.

Prepare the couscous (see *Couscous with seasonal vegetables*). Serve in a dish and arrange the crayfish and pumpkin slices on top.

Flavour and colour contrasts are emphasized in this strongly Moroccan dish.

# Al-cuscus bi-samak al-sultan ibrahim wa qishra al-na'na'
## Couscous with mint-crusted red mullet

Level of difficulty: medium
Preparation time: 30 minutes
Cooking time: 40 minutes

**Serves 4**
*6 red mullet*
*1 bunch mint*
*2 lemons*
*3 limes*
*2 grapefruit*
*Fish stock*
*Oil*

**For the mint crust:**
*100g breadcrumbs*
*50g butter*
*50g flour*
*1/2 bunch mint*

**For the couscous:**
*300g couscous*
*20g butter*
*3 glasses Moroccan tea*

**For the vegetable stock:**
*2 carrots*
*100g radish*
*1 leek*
*1 courgette*
*1 bay leaf*
*1 sprig thyme*
*Ginger*
*Parsley*
*Coriander*

Prepare the couscous (see *Couscous with seasonal vegetables*), but replace the water with three glasses of Moroccan tea (tea bag and mint leaves). Next, prepare the mint crust. Boil the mint in a saucepan for about three minutes. Remove from the heat and plunge into ice-cold water. Drain and pound in a mortar with the butter, flour and breadcrumbs until smooth.

Clean the fish and remove the two fillets. Next, generously coat the skin-side of the fillet with the prepared mint mixture and fry in oil until golden. Remove from the pan. In the same frying pan, quickly fry the peeled and segmented citrus fruits.

When all the components of the dish are ready, arrange the couscous into a pyramid shape into the centre of the dish and place the fillets on top. Arrange the grapefruit, lime and lemon segments around the edge of the dish. Drizzle with vegetable stock (see above).

The coated fish fillets may also be cooked in an ovenproof gratin dish until the crust is browned.

# Kefta bi-l-baid wa-l-tamatim
# Meatballs with eggs and tomato

Level of difficulty: low
Preparation time: 30 minutes
Cooking time: 40 minutes

Serves 4
300g minced beef
200g minced lamb
100g onion
50g ginger
40g cumin
20g garlic
4g salt
6g pepper
7 eggs
2 tablespoons ras el hanout
Flour
Oil
Coriander

For the tomato sauce:
400g chopped tomatoes
100g onion
10g garlic
2 sprigs thyme
Oil

Mix the beef and lamb in a bowl with the salt, pepper, garlic, onion, chopped ginger, three eggs and spices. Leave to marinate for at least 30 minutes. Next, form little balls of meat with the mixture, roll in flour and fry in oil.

For the tomato sauce, sauté the garlic and onion and add the tomato and thyme. Reduce to a thick sauce. When ready, cover the base of a *tajine* dish with the tomato sauce, add the kefta and finally break in an egg. Place in a pre-heated 220°C oven for five minutes.

This dish can be made in the same way with minced chicken.

## Farj mahshu bi-l-sami wa-l-sabib
# Picanton chicken stuffed with couscous and raisins

Level of difficulty: medium
Preparation time: 30 minutes
Cooking time: 25 minutes

**Serves 4**
4 Picanton chickens
Salt

**For the couscous:**
300g couscous
20g butter
3 glasses water
1 teaspoon salt
50g raisins
20g walnuts
1 small onion
1 teaspoon ground cinnamon

First, prepare the couscous (see *Couscous with seasonal vegetables*). When ready, add the raisins, walnuts, cinnamon and fried onion. Remove the giblets and clean the chickens. Salt and stuff with the couscous mixture. Bake in a 220°C oven for about 25 minutes or until the meat is cooked and golden.

This delicious recipe can be prepared with other types of poultry for an equally exquisite result.

Level of difficulty: low
Preparation time: 30 minutes
Cooking time: 5 hours

# *Salila zaur sidi ibrahim bi-l-na'ama*
# Beefsteak with sage

**Serves 4**
*1kg beef sirloin*
*100g butter*
*1 cabbage*
*Salt*

Wash the cabbage and cut into four pieces. Remove the heart and chop finely. Boil for about five minutes. Now drain and poach in butter and salt over a low heat until a puree has been obtained.

**For the meat sauce:**
*Beef trimmings*
*1 l a full bodied red wine*
*50g calf's trotter*
*200g onion, chopped*
*100g carrots*
*1 celery stalk*
*1 bay leaf*
*1 sprig thyme*
*50g sage*
*Salt*

Next prepare the sauce. Lightly fry the meat trimmings until golden. Meanwhile, sauté the chopped onion, calf trotter, carrot, celery, bay leaf and thyme in another pan. Add the meat trimmings, red wine and leave to reduce significantly over a medium heat. When reduced, add the steak, with water and leave to cook for five hours over a low heat. Now remove from the heat, strain the sauce through a sieve and reduce in a pan with the sage until a thick consistency has been reached.

It is typical to flavour sauces with sage in Morocco, especially in beef and lamb roasts.

Level of difficulty: low
Preparation time: 40 minutes
Cooking time: 20 minutes

# *Díb al-bahr muqadur*
# Mogador sea bass

**Serves 4**
*4 portions sea bass*
*600g red peppers*
*150g green peppers*
*150g aubergines*
*150g courgettes*
*100g carrots*
*300g raisins, soaked*
*300g dates*
*2 garlic cloves*

Finely chop the red and green pepper, aubergine, courgette, carrots and dates. Fry the garlic in oil until golden brown over a low heat. Next add the carrots to the pan. After three or four minutes, add the aubergine and courgette. When tender, add the dates and soaked raisins. Set aside.

Clean the sea bass, split it open and remove the bones. Stuff the vegetable mixture between the two fillets and bake in a pre-heated 220°C oven for ten minutes.

Serve with a red pepper *coulis*. To prepare, mix chopped roasted red pepper with salt and cream.

The name of this recipe originates from the old name of Essaouira, a small fishing town on Morocco's Atlantic coast, called Mogador until Morocco's independence in 1956.

Level of difficulty: medium
Preparation time: 20 minutes
Cooking time: 10 minutes

# Ijtinia bi-samida al-sa'fran
# Scallops with couscous and saffron

**Serves 4**
*8 scallops*

**For the couscous:**
*300g couscous*
*20g butter*
*3 glasses water*
*1 teaspoon salt*
*Saffron*

First, prepare the couscous (see *Couscous with seasonal vegetables*), but this time, add the saffron with the butter in the final stage. Clean the scallops and fill with the couscous mixture. Close the shells so they do not open during cooking, and bake in a pre-heated 220°C oven for seven minutes.

Scallops are a delicacy in Morocco and are delicious when served with salted lemons (see *Salad of salted lemon and peppers*).

Level of difficulty: medium
Preparation time: 30 minutes
Cooking time: 45 minutes

# Bastila samak
# Fish *pastilla*

**Serves 4**
*600g rockfish*
*4 sheets* filo *pastry*
*150g onion*
*100g almonds*
*50g parsley*
*50g coriander*
*20g ginger*
*1g saffron*
*2 garlic cloves*
*2 preserved salted lemons*
*3 eggs*
*Fish stock*

Clean the rockfish (red fish or striped bass), fillet and place the meat to one side. Sauté the finely chopped garlic and onion in oil. When golden, add the fish, the chopped saffron, parsley, coriander and ginger. Now add the salted lemons (see *Salad of salted lemon and peppers*), and leave to cook for four or five minutes. Add plenty of fish stock (made from the fish leftovers) and turn off the heat. Leave to cool for approximately fifteen minutes, and carefully remove the lemons and the fish. Add beaten eggs to the mixture.

To make the *pastilla*, cover the base of a mould with two sheets of *filo* pastry, sprinkle with chopped almonds and cover with another layer of pastry. Now add the fish and the egg stock and cover with the final layer of *filo* pastry. Seal the *pastilla* and place into an oven at 220°C for ten minutes.

To make the *pastilla*, it is advisable to use a circular mould.

World Cuisine

# Desserts

Level of difficulty: low
Preparation time: 20 minutes
Cooking time: 5 minutes

# Krib bi-l-'asal al-Atlas
## Crepes with Atlas honey

**Serves 4**

500g very fine semolina
2 eggs
10g dried yeast
10g fresh yeast
100g butter
2 tablespoons honey
1 pinch salt

Mix the semolina, salt, softened butter, eggs and yeasts in a bowl. Beat well until smooth. Break off small balls from the mixture and flatten with greased hands into roughly two millimetre-thick disks. Fry the crepes in a little butter until they are cooked enough to flip over 2 to 3 minutes. Place into an ovenproof dish, drizzle in honey and bake at 220°C for a couple of minutes.

Atlas honey, appreciated for its characteristic taste, is popular throughout Morocco. Crepes are normally served as a dessert, although they may also be eaten for breakfast.

Level of difficulty: medium
Preparation time: 30 minutes
Cooking time: 20 minutes

# *Kura bi- shukulata bi-l-na'na'*
# Chocolate bomb with mint

**Serves 4**
*4 eggs*
*120g caster sugar*
*120g chocolate*
*40g flour*
*70g butter*
*Mint*

Firstly, break the eggs and separate the yolks from the whites. Mix the whites with half the sugar. Beat until soft peaks form. Place a pan on the heat and melt the butter. Now add the grated chocolate. When the chocolate has melted, add the egg yolks, the finely chopped mint and the remaining sugar. Remove from the heat and beat well. Fold the flour and whipped egg white into the mixture. Pour into a large mould or into buttered individual moulds and bake in a pre-heated 220°C oven for about eight minutes.

The chocolate bomb should be crunchy on the outside, and soft and creamy on the inside. The combination of chocolate and mint is perfect, and if a few strips of orange peel are added, the result is impressive.

Level of difficulty: low
Preparation time: 20 minutes
Cooking time: 10 minutes

# Salabiat tuffah-bi-l-'asal
## Apple fritters with honey

**Serves 4**
500g apples
250g flour
2 eggs
200ml milk
50g lemon rind/zest
1 sachet dried yeast
10ml orange flower water
Flaked almonds
Oil
Honey

Blend the flour, eggs, milk, orange flower water and the yeast until a smooth batter has been formed. Next, peel and core the apples using an apple corer, and slice horizontally into 1 centimetre-thick rings. Coat the apple slices in the batter mixture and place into a very hot pan. Fry until golden. Before serving, drizzle with honey and sprinkle with ground almonds.

The apple fritters can also be sprinkled with ground cinnamon or toasted sesame seeds.

Level of difficulty: medium
Preparation time: 30 minutes
Cooking time: 20 minutes

# *Kisa iyyas wa tuffah bi-l-qirfa*
# Pear and apple parcels with cinnamon

**Serves 4**
*1 packet* filo *pastry*
*200g apples*
*200g pears*
*100g sugar*
*50g butter*
*1 tablespoon ground cinnamon*
*Black sesame seeds*

Peel and dice the apples and pears. Heat some butter in a frying pan, add the fruit, sugar and cinnamon and sauté for ten to fifteen minutes. When ready, tip into a fine sieve to drain off the fruit juices. Set aside. Hold the pastry in one palm and spoon a couple of tablespoons of the fruit mixture into the pastry. Close tightly to make a parcel. Place on an ovenproof dish and bake for 220°C for eight minutes.

This dessert may be served dry or drizzled with the reserved fruit juices. It may also be combined with fruit coulis for a delicious result.

Level of difficulty: low
Preparation time: 15 minutes
Cooking time: 2 minutes

# *Yaus wa tamr mashwa*
# Stuffed dates and nuts

Serves 4
*200g dates*
*100g ground almonds*

**For the almond pastry:**
*200g almonds*
*10ml orange flower water*
*50g sugar*
*50g ground cinnamon*
*100g mint leaves*
*200g strawberries, mashed*

Beat the ground almonds, orange flower water, sugar and cinnamon. Divide the mixture in two. Add the strawberries to one half. Mix well. Next, infuse the mint leaves in boiling water for two minutes, take out and place quickly in a glass of ice so they retain their intense green colour. Pulse the leaves with the remaining almond mixture in a blender to make the green filling.

When the two fillings are ready, shape into small balls and stuff into the dates and nuts.

This almond filling is typically used in Moroccan cakes and pastries and can be combined with other ingredients to create other flavours.

# *Tut al-ard al-mamqara bi-l-yasamin*
# Marinated strawberries in orange flower water

Level of difficulty: low
Preparation time: 15 minutes

**Serves 4**
*1kg strawberries*
*100g sugar*
*1 tablespoon balsamic vinegar*
*1 teaspoon orange flower water*
*Juice of 5 oranges*
*4 jasmine flowers*

Wash the strawberries, quarter them and leave to marinate in a bowl with the vinegar, sugar and orange flower water for a couple of hours, or until they have absorbed plenty of liquid. Then add the orange juice and the jasmine flowers and place into the fridge to chill. Serve cold.

This is a simple recipe with the special Moroccan twist of orange flower water and jasmine.

# Authors' selection

## Mohamed Fedal
**Dar Moha Restaurant**
(Marrakech)

Trained initially in the Catering School of Geneva and then professionally in the kitchens of the most prestigious Swiss hotels, Mohamed Fedal returned to his native land after fourteen years of culinary education. In Morocco he established the Dar Moha restaurant, where he rose to show the world the roots of his cooking – a fusion of Moroccan and international cuisine.

## Frédéric Fétiveau
**Medina de Braganza Restaurant**
(Madrid)

Frédéric Fétiveau started his extensive professional career in Paris, where he worked for 10 years in the kitchens of some of the best restaurants of the French capital, all Michelin-star winners. His career continued in Madrid, where he worked in the Hotel Villamagna until 2002, when he became partner and executive director of the Café Oliver, Madrilia, Medina de Braganza and Estik restaurants.

## Fatéma Hal
**Mansouria Restaurant**
(Paris)

Expert in Arabic culture and ethnology, Hal has compiled the most traditional Moroccan recipes, passed down from mother to daughter. In 1984 she opened The Mansouria restaurant in Paris, where she has concentrated on promoting historical Moroccan cuisine, inherited from Berber, Arab-Andalusian, European and even Chinese culture. The dedication to the traditions of her homeland has earned her the prestigious title of ambassador of Moroccan culture.

## Lahida fulful ahmar
Mohamed Fedal | Red pepper purée

**Serves 4**
*3 red peppers*
*1 garlic clove*
*50g flaked almonds*
*1 pinch cumin*
*1 tablespoon lemon juice*
*2 tablespoons sunflower oil*
*Salt*

Clean the peppers, deseed and chop. Pulse in a blender with the garlic and almonds to obtain a purée. Heat some oil in a saucepan and add the purée, cumin, lemon juice and salt to taste. Let the sauce reduce over a low heat, stirring continually, until the liquid has evaporated. Serve cold.

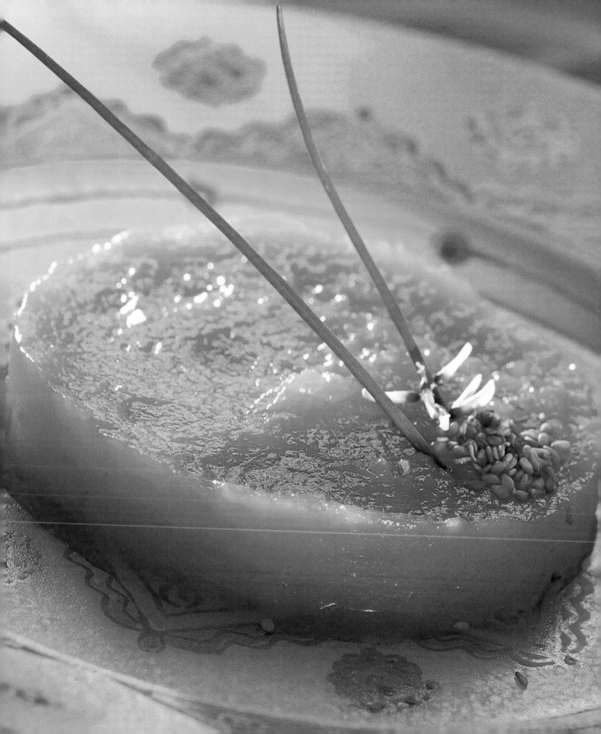

## Mohamed Fedal

# Brick al-summana
# Filo parcels with quail

**Serves 4**
*4 quails*
8 brick or filo *pastry sheets*
*1 onion, chopped*
*30g butter*
*1 tablespoon groundnut oil*
*1 pinch saffron*
*1 teaspoon ground cinnamon*
*1 pinch* ras el-hanout
*Parsley, chopped*
*Coriander, chopped*

Heat the oil in a saucepan and sauté the quail until lightly golden. Remove from the pan. Now add a little coriander, parsley, the onion, cinnamon, *ras el-hanout* (you could substitute a mild curry powder for a less complex effect), butter and saffron. Let the sauce reduce and then return the quail to the pan, breast-side upwards. Leave to cook on a low heat for approximately one hour. Remove and wrap each quail in *filo* sheets. Fry quickly in hot oil and arrange on a dish.

**Presentation**: Arrange the quail on a dish and drizzle in the cooking sauce.

## Mohamed Fedal

# Bastilla farj al-hammama
## Pigeon *pastilla*

**Serves 4**
2 brick *or filo pastry sheets*
*200g pigeon meat*
*4 eggs*
*3 onions*
*150g flaked almonds*
*1 teaspoon ground cinnamon*
*1 tablespoon orange flower water*
*2 glasses pigeon stock*
*200ml oil*
Ras al-hanout
*Ginger*
*Coriander or parsley*
*Saffron*
*Sugar*
*Icing sugar*
*Salt*
*Pepper*
Smen *(clarified butter)*

Season the pigeon with a little salt, pepper, ginger, cinnamon, saffron and *ras el-hanout,* and sauté with *smen* until golden. Add the chopped onions, two glasses of pigeon stock and cook over a low heat until the meat is tender. When cooked, remove from the heat and de-bone. Break the eggs and add to the sauce, stirring with a wooden spoon. Sauté the almonds in a frying pan with a little cinnamon, orange flower water and a pinch of sugar until the mixture has caramelised. Spread a little of the almond mixture over a sheet of *brick* pastry, cover with a layer of pigeon mixture and a layer of the egg sauce, and finally another layer of *brick*. Seal well and fry in hot oil.

**Presentation**: Pigeon pastilla should be served very hot, sprinkled with icing sugar and decorated with flaked almonds.

## Mohamed Fedal

# Shukshuka tuffah bi-l-sa'fran
## Apple shukshuka with saffron

**Serves 4**

*3 golden delicious apples*
*4 sheets* brick *or* filo *pastry*
*50g almonds*
*4 saffron threads*
*1/2 teaspoon ground cinnamon*
*20g butter*
*2 tablespoons sugar*
*40g icing sugar*
*1 tablespoon orange flower water*
*1 tablespoon cornflour*
*200ml milk*
*100ml cream*
*200ml oil*
*Mint*

Peel the apples and dice. Melt the butter in a saucepan and sauté the apples until golden. Add the sugar, cinnamon and saffron and continue to sauté until the apples have caramelised and reduced. Next, cut the *brick* pastry sheets into circles or small squares, according to taste. Fry in a pan of hot oil until golden brown. Remove and place on kitchen paper to absorb excess fat. Toast the almonds, chop and mix with the icing sugar. Place the orange flower water, cornflour, milk and cream in a bowl and whip until frothy. Set aside.

**Presentation**: Layer sheets of the *brick* pastry with the apple mixture, and alternating with the almond mixture. The fragrant whipped cream should be placed in the four corners of the plate. A sprig of fresh mint may be placed on top for decoration.

Frédéric Fétiveau

## *Salata al-burtuqal*
## Orange salad

**Serves 4**
*4 oranges*
*2 grapefruits*
*2 tomatoes*
*1/2 small glass orange flower water*
*1 tablespoon sugar*
*Black olives*
*Olive oil*
*White and black sesame seeds*
*Spring onion*
*Cinnamon*

Peel the oranges and grapefruit and wash the tomatoes. Slice one orange to decorate and finely chop the other three. Do the same with the grapefruit and tomatoes. Mix all the chopped ingredients in a bowl, sprinkle with sugar and add the lemon juice and the orange flower water. Next, add the olives, sprinkle with ground cinnamon and leave to marinate for fifteen minutes. Before serving the salad, drizzle with a little olive oil and sprinkle with chopped spring onion and sesame seeds.

Frédéric Fétiveau

## Al-cuscus bi-l-irbiyan
## Lobster couscous

**Serves 4**
*1kg lobster*
*100g red peppers*
*100g green peppers*
*100g courgettes*
*100g aubergine*
*4 baby carrots*
*Dates*
*Butter*
*Ginger*
*Oil*
*Salt*

**For the couscous:**
*300g couscous*
*20g butter*
*1 teaspoon salt*
*3 glasses water*

**For the vegetable stock:**
*2 carrots*
*100g radish*
*1 leek*
*1 courgette*
*1 bay leaf*
*1 sprig thyme*
*Ginger, parsley and coriander*

Prepare the couscous (see *Couscous with seasonal vegetables*). Boil the lobsters 6 or 7 minutes in salted water until cooked. Cut lengthways and remove the meat. Set aside. Place the shells, heads and claws in another bowl. Finely cut the green and red pepper, courgette, dates, aubergine and ginger. Poach the vegetables until *al dente* in a saucepan with a little oil, season and stuff into the lobster shells.

Boil the baby carrots in a pan of salted water. Remove when cooked, drain and sauté quickly with the lobster meat and a knob of butter. Make a mound of couscous on the plates and arrange with the lobster sauce, the stuffed shells, the lobster heads and claws.

Frédéric Fétiveau

## Fajd al-jaruf bi-l-'asal wa-l-burtuqal
## Leg of suckling lamb with honey and orange

**Serves 4**
*2 legs suckling lamb*
*1/2 l orange juice*
*100g orange compote*
*300g onion, chopped*
*1 orange, peeled and chopped*
*50g garlic, chopped*
*20g cumin*
*50g sesame seeds*
*1g saffron*
*1g honey*
*Meat stock*
*Oil*
*Salt*

Place the garlic and onion in a saucepan and lightly fry with a little oil until golden. Add the legs of lamb, cumin, saffron and the orange juice. Place a lid over the pan and leave to cook over a low heat for five minutes, stirring from time to time to stop the mixture sticking to the bottom. Next, cover with meat stock; add the honey, orange compote and orange flesh, and place into the oven for one hour thirty minutes, adding a little more stock to the mixture from time to time if necessary. When the lamb is golden and cooked through, remove from the oven and serve sprinkled with toasted sesame seeds.

Frédéric Fétiveau

## *Tamatim marqada bi-l-tut al-ard*
## Caramelised tomatoes with raspberries

**Serves 4**
*8 tomatoes*
*200g sugar*
*100g frozen raspberries*
*Mint*

Blanch the tomatoes in boiling water for one minute. Remove the skins and immediately place into a bowl of iced water. Using a spoon, make a hole in one side of the tomato and scrape out the seeds.

Bring a pan to the boil with a little water. Add the sugar and mint and continue cooking on high heat for ten minutes. Remove from the heat, add the cold tomatoes and coat in the caramelised sugar syrup until it has turned cold. To finish, stuff the tomatoes with raspberries and serve chilled.

Fatéma Hal

# Asabi' al-'arusa: Lafat bi'-l-irbiyan
## Prawn rolls

**Serves 4**
**For the filling:**
*250g peeled prawns*
*2 spoonfuls oil*
*3 garlic cloves, peeled and crushed*
*1 tomato, peeled and chopped*
*1 green pepper, chopped*
*1/2 teaspoon salt*
*1/2 teaspoon cumin*
*Juice of 1/2 lemon*
*Coriander, chopped*
*Oil*

**For the pastry:**
*12* brick *or* filo *pastry sheets*
*1 egg yolk*

**The filling**: Heat two spoonfuls of oil in a pan over a high heat and add the garlic, coriander, salt, cumin and lemon juice. Fry lightly for approximately three minutes, stirring continually with a wooden spoon. Lower the heat and add the chopped tomatoes. After seven minutes, add the prawns and green pepper. Three or four minutes later, remove from the heat and cool.

**The pastry**: Cut the *filo* pastry sheets in two. Place a spoonful of filling onto each sheet and roll up into a finger shape. Seal with a little beaten egg yolk and fry in plenty of oil for five minutes until golden. Serve hot.

## Fatéma Hal

### *Mawrusiyya*
### Lamb stew with raisins and almonds

**Serves 4**
*1kg cubed lamb*
*2 onions, chopped*
*300g raisins*
*2 teaspoons* ras el hanout
*100g honey*
*500ml water*
*1 tablespoon* smen *(clarified butter)*
*2 tablespoons groundnut oil*
*1/2 teaspoon salt*
*1/2 teaspoon pepper*
*Saffron threads*

Melt 20g butter very slowly and pour off the clarified butter, leaving the sediment behind. Mix the salt, pepper, a few saffron threads, *ras el hanout* and 100ml water in a bowl. Generously coat the meat with half the mixture and place in a metal casserole dish with the oil, remaining water, onion, clarified butter (*smen*) and the skinned almonds. Heat over a low heat for 45 minutes; meanwhile, soak the raisins in warm water, and when slightly swollen, drain and add to the meat with the remaining spices. Cook slowly for a further 20 minutes, add the honey and continue cooking until the almonds and raisins have caramelised.

**Presentation**: Serve hot and sprinkle with a few raisins and almonds to decorate.

## Bastilla halib
## Milk *pastilla*

Fatéma Hal

**Serves 4**

*12* brick *or* filo *pastry sheets*
*500g almonds*
*150g sugar*
*1/2 litre milk*
*1/2 tablespoon orange flower water*
*100g butter*
*2 tablespoons groundnut oil*

Peel the almonds and toast in a frying pan with a little oil. Remove and place on kitchen paper to remove the excess fat. Crush in a mortar. Add the sugar, mix well and set aside. Next, melt the butter in a pan and fry the *brick* sheets two by two until golden. Place the first two sheets in a dish and spread with the almond mixture. Continue layering the *brick* pastry sheets with the sugared almond mixture until the dish is full. Finally, pour the milk and orange flower water into a pan and heat for a few seconds on a low heat.

**Presentation**: Just before serving, drizzle orange-flavoured milk over the *pastilla*.

# Ka'b al-ghazal wa halwiyat tamar wa 'asal

## Gazelle horns with date and honey cakes

Fatéma Hal

Serves 4-6

**For the almond pastry:**
*1kg skinned almonds*
*500g caster sugar*
*2 tablespoons orange flower water*
*1 tablespoon melted butter*

**For the gazelle horn pastry:**
*500g flour*
*1 tablespoon butter*
*100ml orange flower water*

**For the cake paste:**
*1kg honey*
*750g semolina (mix of fine and medium-grained)*
*250g melted butter*
*100g caster sugar*
*1 teaspoon ground cinnamon*
*1 teaspoon ground cubeb pepper*
*2 tablespoons orange flower water*
*Salt*

**For the cake filling:**
*1kg dates, stoned*
*100g sesame seeds*
*1 teaspoon cinnamon*
*1/2 teaspoon ground cubeb*
*1/2 tablespoon butter*

**The almond pastry:** Blend the almonds and sugar. Add the orange flower water, melted butter and mix. Make little balls, gently pressing and shaping them into cylindrical forms.

**The gazelle horns:** Mix all the ingredients to form an even pastry. Roll out some of the pastry extremely finely. Place the almond shapes on the pastry, fold over and shape into a croissant or half-moon, seal the edges and trim. Indent with a knife along the join, brush with egg white and bake for 10 minutes, until lightly golden.

**The semolina cake paste:** Place the semolina in a bowl, make a hole in the centre and pour in the melted butter, honey, spices, sugar and salt. Mix together to form a pastry. Leave to cool in a fridge overnight.

**The date filling:** Steam the dates for 30 minutes, stirring occasionally. Place into a bowl and mash to a paste. Add the sesame seeds, cinnamon, *cubeb* pepper and the melted butter. Continue mixing. Leave to cool. When ready, shape into long cylinders. Set aside.

**The cakes:** Mix the orange flower water with a pinch of salt. Pour a little of this liquid into the semolina paste. Mix well and roll gently into a cylindrical form. Introduce the date filling. Seal and flatten. Cut into diamond shapes and fry in plenty of oil. Drain on kitchen paper. In a bowl, mix a little honey and orange flower water and drizzle over the cakes.

# Drinks

Mint tea is not only the national drink of Morocco and other North African countries: drinking tea in cafés is a most enjoyable social pass-time, and one that is especially favoured by male members of the population, as well as being considered a symbol of hospitality. Furthermore, good quality wine is still produced today, beer is also brewed and natural fruit juices are abundant.

Tea introduced by the British married well with traditional Moroccan tisanes, and has become an essential element of Moroccan daily life. Moroccans enjoy relaxing with a glass of tea in grand cafés or at home after a day's work.

## Mint tea

Tea is traditionally infused with mint leaves to intensify its refreshing qualities in Morocco, Algeria, Tunisia and Egypt. Moroccan *'thé à la menthe'*, one Moroccan culinary element that has retained its French name, is prepared with China tea, fresh mint, boiling water and sugar. The tea is brewed in metal teapots and served in small glasses. To retain its intense flavour, it is poured in two stages, and from a great height, to make it frothy on top and to obtain its light golden colour. Often, Moroccan towns have a number of finely decorated cafés purely for tea drinking. These cafés, decked out with plenty of comfortable armchairs, are the perfect spot to relax while drinking a mint tea and smoking a *nargile*, or water pipe filled with different flavoured tobacco. Indulging in a tasty Moroccan pastry or sweet is popular, too. In these cafés, all kinds of coffee are also served, ranging from the more traditional western style coffees to flavoured and spiced Moroccan varieties. Tea has become the hallmark of the Arabic tradition of hospitality, and refusing it is considered a sign of poor education. The utensils used for making tea, including the teapot and glasses, form part of Moroccan craftwork, and are intricately decorated with various Arabic motifs. Tea can also be drunk with other aromatic herbs, although none is more popular and revered as mint tea.

## Wine

Although Islam prohibits the drinking of alcohol, wine and beer is widely available in Morocco, although Moroccans maintain a fairly prudent and discrete attitude towards drinking it. The proximity of the Mediterranean and the Atlantic, the warm climate and the protection given by the Altas Mountains provides the perfect environment for wine production. The French exploited these characteristics – firstly in Algeria, and wines were produced here for export. However, with Algeria's independence, wine production, which at that time was half the world's wine supply, fell significantly. Now, there are a few coastal areas that concentrate on producing quality wines rather than producing for quantity.

Today in Morocco, there are about 15,000 hectares of working vineyards and a dozen DO wines (Morocco follows the French model of quality certification for wines). The greatest wine production area is around the cities of Meknès and Fez, and in the Atlas Mountain foothills, where good rosé from Cinsault, Carignena, Garnacha and Syrah grapes is produced. Another noteworthy region is that which lies between Casablanca and Rabat, where *Vin Gris* white wine is made, which must be served chilled. Other than these wines, the majority of Moroccan wine is rough and with high alcohol content, and is often mixed with European wines to obtain a

smoother blend. In the rest of North Africa, there is a great variety of Tunisian Moscatels, and in Algeria, a number of strong and dry wines are produced, where loss of a powerful industry has been compensated by more modest yet better-quality wine.

### Beer

Compared to the up-market tradition of drinking wine, beer is the most popular alcoholic drink in Morocco. The best-known makes are produced by the Société des Brasseries du Maroc, founded in 1919, which has turned beer consumption into an accessible activity. Nowadays, Moroccan produced beer is favoured over the large number of imported makes.

### Natural fruit juices

It is quite common to find freshly squeezed fruit juices in Moroccan towns and cities; some may be flavoured with orange flower water or cinnamon. Pomegranate, watermelon and grape juice are also common. *Sharbat* is another popular drink made from milk or buttermilk and is mixed with almond juice, avocado and other fresh fruit juices.

# Index